Things I Wish I'd Known

When I Started My Career

Advice, Wisdom and Insights for Young Professionals

MIDVALE PRESS

For Patrick

Things I Wished I'd Known When I Started My Career

"To profit from good advice requires more wisdom than to give it."

- Wilson Mizner

"... take advice from other folks, use what you can, but never mind what is not for you."

- Musiq Soulchild

Midvale Press
400 South Elliott Road
Suite 136-D
Chapel Hill, N.C. 27514

isbn#: 978-1-7363756-8-6

LCCN#: 2024903054

First Edition

Printed and bound in the United States of America

10 9 8 7 6 5 4 3 2 1

MIDVALE PRESS

Table of Contents

ATTITUDE

Things I Wished I'd Known When I Started My Career

Believe in yourself

If you don't, success is nearly impossible

Trust yourself

Doubt offers important warnings, but don't let it run the show

Give others the respect you desire

*Everything is a two-way street.
(It's not all about you)*

Be forward-looking

Historical context is important
but focus your efforts on the future

Be solution-oriented

Too many people focus on the problem; focus on the solution...or better yet, several possible solutions

Don't resent small assignments

They will lead to bigger assignments if you do three things: 1) accept them eagerly; 2) treat them as opportunities to demonstrate your abilities; and 3) knock it out of the park

Commit

*Fully commit to the process and to
doing the best job possible
regardless of how you feel about it*

Be positive

Negativity is easy, cheap, off-putting and counter-productive. If you find positivity to be a challenge in a particular situation, aim for neutrality

Be polite; recognize that manners are incredibly important

Manners are simply a social convention to make life easier for everyone; those who possess them move up quickly

Be easygoing and someone people want to be around

Intensity is a small-dose attribute, best applied sparingly; as a steady diet it wears people out

Be forgiving

*You will need it yourself at times,
so pass it around*

Don't be judgmental

...lest you be judged

Don't be self-absorbed

A self-absorbed person is tiresome to others. You're not the only one in the room

Never complain. And never, _ever_ whine

Whiners have a short-shelf life

Never make excuses

Excuses make you look weak.
Admit you screwed up and go on

Learn to let things go

Things accumulate. If you don't let them go, you will be carrying too much weight to move forward

Smile – it creates endorphins and hence becomes a self-fulfilling prophecy

If you spend more time on gratitude, your smile will be more genuine

Don't seek to justify your existence by appearing stressed, overworked, and exhausted

*People avoid colleagues and don't
follow leaders who are stressed
out and harried*

Let your work speak for itself

If you have to point and posture,
your work is likely sub-par

See the glass as half full

...because it is

If you're in a bad mood, be quiet, keep to yourself, and smile anyway

Mood swings are unbecoming and counter-productive in the workplace

Continually build your network

Tend your network like a garden: constantly cultivate your friends and colleagues because meaningful, accessible contacts will expire without attention

Measure prospective new assignments, positions and jobs in terms of opportunity, not dollars

Dollars will follow opportunity

Never do things grudgingly; even if you do them well, you won't get the next assignment

People go out of their way to avoid working with someone with a bad attitude

Be professional (1)

Deliver the same consistent, high-level performance every day in every situation regardless of your mood, health or circumstances

Be professional (2)

*Keep home and personal issues out
of the work place*

CULTIVATE YOUR BRAND

Things I Wished I'd Known When I Started My Career

Establish yourself as someone who is professional...in action *and* attitude

<u>*Always!*</u>
A brand is only a brand if it is consistent

Demonstrate a can-do attitude

*No need to be annoyingly upbeat.
A quiet confidence and a
pleasant demeanor will do*

Establish yourself as someone who will "get it done"

Ultimately, that's the only thing anyone cares about

Be known as someone who finishes the job

Keep finishing jobs satisfactorily and on time and those jobs will proliferate and grow

Understand that timeliness is critical

Don't rationalize lateness. It's not acceptable

Be organized.
Keep it together.
Be calm

Excitable, panicky, hotheads go nowhere. You can train yourself to be calm

CRITICAL WORK HABITS

Things I Wished I'd Known When I Started My Career

Find mentors

Mentors are critical to your professional growth, come in all shapes and sizes, and are both official and unofficial

Watch and listen (1)

*Better to keep your mouth shut
and be thought a fool than to open
it and remove all doubt*

Watch and listen (2)

You don't learn anything when you're talking

Be discreet

If you are told something in confidence, NEVER pass it on

Make a habit of keeping your eyes open and your mouth shut

You will learn more if people know you don't talk

Be comprehensive – tend assiduously to the details

If you have not provided the details, very often you might as well have not done anything at all

Avoid sloppiness at all costs – double and triple check your work

Sloppiness is a career-killer

If you're going to communicate a problem, propose a solution

Nobody wants a problem; they want solutions

Under-promise and over-deliver

Classic advice...and still golden

Title: On the Electrodynamics of Moving Bodies

Show Up

*You can beat 80% of the people
simply by showing up*

Persevere

*If you can beat 80% of the people
simply by showing up, you can beat
another 15% with staying power*

Adopt the 15% Rule

Add 15% to every estimate when anticipating effort, complexity, time or cost

Fast...Good...Cheap

Pick two

Pick your battles

People appreciate a fighter, but someone who is constantly combative is just a pain in the ass

Stay off your cellphone and social media in the office

There's work to be done. Grow up!

Remember the name of
new acquaintances going forward.
Repeat their name back to them
and then take a minute to burn
it into your mind

*Knowing someone's name in subsequent
meetings will earn you respect and
appreciation. Remembering and asking
about a personal detail wouldn't hurt either*

Don't let perfect be the enemy of good

If it's worth doing, it's worth doing half-assed...if that's all that time or circumstance allow

If you can produce "excellent" instead of just "good"...do so!

The difference is usually aggressive polishing at the end

Do it now

Procrastinate later

Be aware of where any given activity falls in the Eisenhower matrix

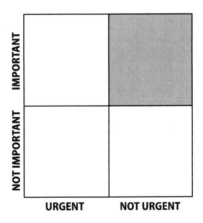

Plan well to avoid imminent tasks crowding out important ones

Follow up, follow up, follow up

People do what you <u>in</u>spect, not what you <u>ex</u>pect

If you're not five minutes early, you're late

Plan as if the meeting begins 10 minutes before it really does...and then assume there will be a delay in getting there

Don't be afraid to ask for help

Asking also leads to relationships

Ask superiors, colleagues and clients about themselves

The more you listen, the more they think you understand

If there is a solution, find it; if not, drop it

Sometimes there isn't a solution; tell your ego to deal with it and move on

Understand and respect the opposing opinion

If you don't understand it, you can't counter it

Apologize once and move on

Once is appropriate; beyond that, nobody has time for obsequiousness

Stick to your guns

Until you realize you're wrong...then throw down your guns cheerfully

Avoid knee-jerk reactions

*Wait until they are fully formed
before voicing them in public*

In the face of injustice or unfair treatment, bide your time

Injustice and unfairness often self-destruct; if they don't, a well thought out and timely response will serve best

Never name the first number in a negotiation

Make the other person show their hand first

Practice success and failure mode planning (pre-thinking responses to likely outcomes, good or bad)

Things will almost certainly not turn out exactly as you planned...so be prepared for the most likely eventualities

Be efficient with incidentals to make time for more important things

The client awaiting your call doesn't care if your paper clips are neatly sorted

Don't major in minor things

Some things matter; others don't (at least not much). Strive to work on what matters

Minimize busy-ness

*Don't confuse it with work...it's
usually the opposite*

Do things you don't like first and get them out of the way

You can waste the whole day avoiding unpleasant tasks

Don't make assumptions

Too often they will be wrong

Be aware when you *are* making assumptions (which is more often than you think)

Too often people are certain they know something <u>without even realizing</u> it is merely an assumption

Take time to brainstorm

It often happens away from the office...in the hammock...on a walk. It may be the most valuable thinking you do. Create space for it

Don't be afraid to have nine bad ideas before finding the tenth good one

Just don't loudly champion the first thing that comes to your mind (See Thomas Edison)

Pursue and maintain contacts outside your company

They may be valuable to your company while you are there...and even more so to you after you leave

Don't be concerned that
you have no idea how a
new acquaintance fits
into what you are doing
at the moment...

Things change

Put the effort into maintaining professional relationships

You will need them

Eat protein at breakfast; eat a light lunch

The protein in the breakfast will carry you through the morning...a heavy lunch will make you sleepy in the afternoon

Share your successes when appropriate, but never, ever brag

There is a proper time for everything...except for off-putting, gratuitous braggadocio, either by word or attitude

Things I Wished I'd Known When I Started My Career

WORKING WITH
OTHERS

Things I Wished I'd Known When I Started My Career

Treat everyone with utmost respect

There is no profit in not treating people well. And the people you meet going up may be the same ones you meet going down

Spread credit very generously

Especially when you feel inclined to brag.
A rising tide lifts all boats

Poor planning by you does not constitute an emergency for someone else...and vice versa

Take responsibility for your own mess; help others out with theirs if you can

Give people the benefit of the doubt (until they no longer deserve it)

You rarely know ALL the facts...so don't risk looking the fool by acting like you do

Don't blame; just move forward

Whether public or private, blame is rarely the most productive action

"See" people

*And let them know you are
seeing them*

Practice deep listening

It's the opposite of casual listening

Ask questions about others; avoid talking about yourself

In addition to being thought of as a great conversationalist, you will learn something

Don't hold grudges

It is a waste of time and energy and impedes progress...mostly your own

Recognize the team is greater than the sum of its parts

Even key personnel are diminished without colleagues

Keep business and personal matters separate

*Business and personal matters –
especially romance and finance – are
messy when co-mingled*

Office friendships are fine, but in the office keep them business-like

Acting in a business-like fashion advances the business and does not compromise the friendship. Friendships can be resumed after hours (See "Be professional")

Avoid office politics and office gossip

It belittles everyone; real players sail above it

Avoid office romance

...like the plague!

Strive to make colleagues be better and look better

It will build teamwork and come back to you three-fold

Don't take issue with or waste time on ancillary matters

Sometimes the annoying paperwork just needs to be done. Don't fight it. Don't bitch about it. Just do it efficiently and get back to more important things

Don't be afraid to say, "I don't know," "I'll look into it," or 'I'll get back to you on that"

You're not supposed to know everything; you look like a fool if you try to look like you do

Prepare by understanding the other person's perspective

You need to know where someone is coming from

Don't confuse someone's perspective with their idea or opinion

Suspect ideas often come from perfectly valid perspectives. Try not to reject the perspective just because the idea is imperfect

Recognize hidden agendas...including your own

They almost always exist...and usually they're not nefarious. Those who possess them often don't realize it themselves

Be careful about challenging hidden agendas

If they are nefarious you will be in a dogfight; if they are not, people will feel attacked. Awareness of someone else's hidden agenda requires a thoughtful and often strategic response; open challenge is rarely the best course

Sometimes challenging someone's hidden agenda is *absolutely* the right course

Decide whether a public or private challenge is best. Then call them out

Strive to align agendas

The goal is always win-win, but the path to that is aligning everyone's agenda around the same outcome

Things I Wished I'd Known When I Started My Career

ALL
COMMUNICATION

Things I Wished I'd Known When I Started My Career

Be succinct

It's one of the most useful skills you can learn...and you will be appreciated for it

Strive for clarity and transparency

The point of all communication

Learn to find the nub of the matter

Try to avoid anyone ever asking you,
"So what's the point?"

Get to the point
Make the point
Stay on point
Then shut up

The opposite of rambling

Think before speaking or writing

Always. And for 24 hours if you can

Communicate in digestible bits

Make sure your listener gets your point before moving to the next one

Pitch your ideas strategically

Put as much energy into crafting your delivery as you did in developing your idea in the first place

Know your audience

Unless people see what's in it for them – usually accolades, advancement or a possible bonus – even good ideas will be met with disinterest as just one more thing to do

Understand that revolutionary ideas are always met with skepticism...or they are not revolutionary

If more than two people out of ten "get it" the first time you explain it, your idea is not as revolutionary as you thought

Don't preach to the choir

If you are not presenting them with an action request, they will consider you to be wasting their time

ORAL
PRESENTATIONS

Things I Wished I'd Known When I Started My Career

Speak more slowly than you think you should

Audiences need time to digest what you are saying

Repeat yourself

*Tell them what you're going to say...
say it...and then tell them what
you just said*

Pause frequently

*Pausing and looking at various parts
of the audience emphasizes the important
point you just made and implies they
need to absorb it before you move on*

Speak directly to three random people in different sections of the audience rather than the whole audience

It will de-escalate the tension for you and it will personalize the delivery as every person in that section will think you are speaking to them

Smile

In small presentations and large, if you can smile naturally it will relax everyone, including you, and improve audience receptivity

Number your points

Numbering your points helps listeners organize the information in their heads. Three numbered points are best; six is usually the max

Learn to speak well

Get a coach. Learn to understand voice modulation. Become aware of your annoying accent, your nasal tone, or bad speech habits, like repeatedly saying "you know". Learn to speak in short, clear sentences

Take a public speaking course

...or join Toastmasters or a similar organization. Not being able to present adequately will hold you back

WRITTEN
COMMUNICATION

Things I Wished I'd Known When I Started My Career

Learn to Write

*Your ideas are only as good as your
ability to communicate them*

Put any requested action at the very top of the email or memo

People often don't read past the first sentence or two

Use executive summaries

It's time saver for the reader, and constructing it will help you find the nub of the matter for later discussion

Avoid the passive voice

It's weak

Use bullet points

People read bullet points far more readily than paragraphs

Be generous with white space

A page full of copy exhausts the eye

Put long explanations or secondary information in footnotes or addenda

In the main narrative they just clutter up the point...and people will stop reading

Draft and re-draft until you are polishing

It is the polishing that raises a presentation from good to excellent...and excellence makes all the difference in the outcome

Hold angry memos and letters for one day before sending

Put it in your desk drawer or save file for a day or longer. There is a 99% chance you won't send or will edit it

Less is usually more

*Find the simplest way to say it.
Then stop*

LEADERSHIP

Things I Wished I'd Known When I Started My Career

Have a vision

A vision is a leader's most important tool

Be able to communicate your vision

If you can't, it is of no use

Lead by example

*Actions speak louder than words;
a cliché, but true*

Be clear in your expectations of others

People have to know what you expect of them. You have to know it first

Make sure everyone understands the objective

Both for the team and for themselves

Know your people as people, not just as employees

It will build loyalty if your team knows you also recognize them as people with lives of their own

It is difficult for employees to be friends

Some distance is usually necessary if you are to lead

Be aggressively inclusive

The only acceptable criterion for exclusion is performance

Be sincere

Even if you don't mean it 😐

Ask for people's input

Not only will it be helpful, but they will know you value their insight

Make it about the team, not about you

People don't want to work for your advancement; they want to work for their own

Take responsibility

The most basic requirement of a leader

Deploy people thoughtfully, matching their skills with the job

The wrong person in the wrong job can scuttle the whole enterprise

Be generous in mentoring others

It's in your own best interest...and it will come back to you

Be thoughtful

People want to know you've thought things through and are doing things a certain way for a reason. (You don't always have to explain it)

Be decisive

Pull the trigger! It's usually easier to recover from a mistake than it is from wishy-washiness, missed opportunities and perceived weakness

Be flexible if you can

There are often extenuating circumstances. The more you allow for those which are legitimate, the more people will follow you

Take the long view

That is the leader's role – to orchestrate action in service to the long-term vision

Recognize when the short term supersedes the long view

If you can't make next month's numbers for the third time in a row, the long view suddenly becomes less important. Better switch your priorities temporarily

Surround yourself with people who are smarter than you are and / or know more than you do

They exist (in abundance). Accept it. It's the quickest and best way to get the job done

You can't always know all the answers, but strive to know the right questions

Quit trying to know everything and focus instead on knowing where to look, and how to extract the information in real time

Know who knows the answers to various questions...and keep those people on speed dial

This is your "kitchen cabinet" –
at least for information

Find a ground-truther

Someone wise and experienced whom you can talk with, whose judgment you trust and who has institutional memory. Ideally this person will not have a stake in the issue at hand

Find the win-win solution

It's usually there. You may have to craft things a bit, but its more than worth the trouble

Find the best people and trust them

*You can't micro-manage good people
or you won't have them for long*

Learn to delegate

But again...recognize that people do what you <u>in</u>spect not what you expect

Don't expect others to do things you wouldn't

If you do, you may quickly meet resentment that will thwart the entire enterprise

Pitch in sometimes

Your willingness to work shoulder to shoulder inspires loyalty

If someone on your team is failing, take personal responsibility as their superior before assigning blame

Sit down with them and ask them what <u>you</u> are not doing to help them succeed

Encourage blue sky brainstorming sessions in which all ideas are accepted and criticism or judgment is forbidden

The interaction is bonding, people get excited and inspired, and the thinking that comes out of it usually provides new directions. Impractical or bad ideas will fall aside organically as the process unfolds

Seek out those who are wise as well as those who are smart

There's a big difference. Learn to recognize it

Find a way to give the rogue genius his or her freedom to create – without upsetting others

Foster and reward genius with freedom to create, but keep an eye out for team resentment

Curate institutional memory in people and in data

Learn who has it. It's a valuable resource for leadership and decision-making

Create retreats and organic bonding opportunities

The break from the day-to-day routine can result in great group creativity

Beware of bogus team-building exercises

Team-bonding and trust building is important, but it's best achieved organically rather than through artificial trust falls and treasure hunts

Create unlikely pairings in mini-teams

It will strengthen the team, build relationships, and help people grow by pushing them outside their comfort zones

Consider having an empty conference room without furniture

You'd be surprised how quickly people get to the business at hand if they can't sit around, nurse a coffee and doodle on a pad of paper

Things I Wished I'd Known When I Started My Career

GIVING BACK

You have worked hard to get where you are, but others have almost certainly helped you along the way

Be grateful by paying it forward with a percentage of your time or money

How much you give is not as important as *that* you give

Treat your financial donations like your investment – pull a certain percentage out before you start creating a monthly budget, then work with what's left. If your contributions are your time, schedule it in advance

Focus the time or money you give away on causes that matter to you

Giving out of joy and passion and caring is one of the most important things you can do...for yourself!

Be strategic on how you give your time or money

Giving consistently to one or two causes will likely do more good than giving a little bit here and there to many causes

Recognize opportunities to make a difference

They are everywhere; simply training yourself to look for them will make you a better, less self-absorbed person

Don't apologize for what you earn or have

...provided you use it as a tool to help others and not just as a prop for your ego

Understand your own philanthropic impulses and activities

Make sure they emanate from sincerity and from your heart, and not simply to appear generous or to seek a tax deduction

Unless you are headed to the hospital, never pass up the chance to stop and buy from a child selling lemonade

There is nothing so important or so rewarding as supporting or inspiring a young person

Ultimately, life is about giving back, paying it forward and creating a better world

To a large extent, the quality of your life will be determined by your own generosity...or your own selfishness

GENERAL WISDOM

Things I Wished I'd Known When I Started My Career

Find your passion

Then find someone to pay you to do it

If you love what you do, you'll never work a day in your life

But there will always be annoying paperwork. Accept it

You have one reputation; *never, ever* compromise it

And don't *talk about* it...just don't do anything to damage it

Your integrity is priceless

If you compromise your integrity, you are the one setting a low value on yourself. Others will follow suit

The only question to ask of every circumstance is not "Why me?" but rather, "What can I be learning from this?"

Life is a learning experience, but the learning is optional. Try to learn from everyone, no matter how low on the totem pole, and every circumstance, no matter how small

Recognize that setbacks are part of the journey – and maybe the most valuable part

Don't resent them. Appreciate the lessons they offer

Setbacks aren't the only teachers

Take particular time to search for cautionary tales hiding inside your successes

The universe is not out to get you

...it's just unfolding

Value is subjective

*Things are only good or bad
because you define them as such –
a truth which gives you more
power and control than you realize*

Usually it's not about you

*It's just not. Adopt a more
humble perspective*

Don't expect your job or your career to bring ultimate fulfillment

That can only come from within yourself. Looking elsewhere will only bring disappointment and bitterness

Save First

Don't make saving a line item in your budget or you will drop it. Treat it like tax withholding by putting your first dollars every pay period – either through company direct deposit or as a matter of discipline – into your savings vehicle. And then budget with what's left

Save Early

Even though it is more difficult to save when you are starting out, recognize that compounding interest makes early dollars many times more valuable than later dollars. At 7% annual interest, every $100 invested when you are 21 is worth about $1600 when you are 66; that same $100 invested when you are 45 is worth only about $400 at age 66

Learn to quiet your mind

Then spend part of each day in quiet

Learn to be comfortable with solitude

Solitude can recharge your batteries and open the door to the still, small, voice inside

Recognize that you are at once utterly inconsequential in the larger scheme of things AND of limitless value to the universe

Both are true, but part of your journey is finding your own way to understand and reconcile this apparent contradiction

Take care of yourself, physically, emotionally, mentally, and spiritually

*Otherwise you won't be any good
to anybody else*

Get out of your own head

If you are thinking 24 hours a day, or see thinking as the only way to arrive at a solution, then you are over-thinking

Don't trust the voice in your head. In fact...shut it down a large percentage of the time

Use your mind as an analytical tool when needed. The rest of the time don't let it create fictional narratives and worst-case scenarios that usually have little basis in fact and always distract you from living in the present

Develop your intuition

Intuition is often far more reliable than your thoughts

Embrace the present moment

*The present is the only moment you have.
If you are angry, you are living in the past;
if you are worried, you are living in the
future. On a practical basis, neither exist,
so if you are not in the present, you are
in fantasy land*

Schedule leisure

This is not only allowed but encouraged. Escape from debilitating workaholism by making leisure time a priority and scheduling work around it

Strive for honest humility

All you have to do is realize all you have to be humble about

Guard against false humility

Humble-bragging is tiresome. People see it for what it is

You do not need to justify your existence: you are enough as you are

The universe is not your landlord and does not require achievement as rent. You are here by invitation.

If you work for yourself, you are fully exposed to any business downturn, but...

No company will ever place as high a priority on your career interests as you will

If you work for someone else, never become complacent. No matter how much people seem to value you, you are at any given minute completely expendable

The company's survival – or sometimes just the bottom line – is a higher priority to the company than any individual – even the CEO

Your best chance at job security is excellence, effort and a strategy to make yourself as indispensable as possible

And preferably all three

Be realistic: Recognize both your power and your limitations

And know that exceptions to both are often the rule

In terms of both time and money, understand that you are always either investing or spending

There is a time for both but make sure you are intentional about which you are doing at any one time

Face your fears

They intimidate and grow when avoided; they diminish or dissolve when confronted

Do those things you are avoiding first

The rest of your day will be much more pleasant and productive

Recognize the power of habit

It takes three days to develop a bad habit,
and thirty days to develop a healthy new one.
But thirty days is a small discomfort
compared to the reward

Things I Wished I'd Known When I Started My Career

Be genuine

Alternatively, don't be phony. Ever!

Be yourself

Still the best advice ever given

Things I Wished I'd Known When I Started My Career

Tim Troupe Noonan

Tim Troupe Noonan has spent nearly 50 years in business, media, academia, not-for-profits, and consulting. He has served as founder, president, go-fer, and at every level in between, and served in every corporate culture from friendly to toxic.